DARE TO
LEAD

Other books by Byrd Baggett:

The Book of Excellence
Satisfaction Guaranteed
The Pocket Power Book series
The Complete Book of Business Success
Power Serve
Dare to Soar
The Soul of Winning
The Past Doesn't Have a Future, But You Do

DARE TO LEAD

Proven Principles
of Effective Leadership

BYRD BAGGETT

CUMBERLAND HOUSE
NASHVILLE, TENNESSEE

Published by
CUMBERLAND HOUSE PUBLISHING, INC.
431 Harding Industrial Drive
Nashville, TN 37211

Cover design: Gore Studio, Inc.
Text design: Lisa Taylor

Library of Congress Cataloging-in-Publication Data
Baggett, Byrd.
    [Taking charge]
    Dare to lead : proven principles of effective leadership /
Byrd Baggett.
        p. cm.
    Previously published as: Taking charge. Nashville, Tenn. :
Rutledge Hill Press, ©1995. With new introd.
    ISBN 1-58182-426-2 (hardcover)
1. Leadership. 2. Quality of work life. I.Title.
    HD57.7.B34 2004
    658.4'092—dc22
ISBN:978-1-684-42395-8   2004018747

2 3 4 5 6 7 8 — 09 8 07 06

To the brave men and women of the Armed Forces of the United States of America, who willingly risk their lives so that all Americans and citizens of the world may enjoy the wonderful fruits of freedom. They are the true heroes, as their courage and sacrifice keep the flame of hope burning. May God continue to bless and protect each soldier.

Introduction

My expertise is helping organizations build and sustain cultures of sales and service excellence. I have earned the distinction as America's Culture Coach by sharing the knowledge, skills, and inspiration that have proven to inspire personal accountability, improve employee morale, and increase bottom-line profitability. My "Dare to Lead" message has been presented to many Fortune 500 companies and has helped hundreds of managers become more effective in their leadership roles. The purpose of this book is to share these practical and applicable insights and strategies that—when applied—will help you become a more effective leader, both at work and at home.

My books have received considerable international recognition and I am honored that others are interested in my common-sense insights. As I travel and visit with people across the country, there remains one constant—people are lonely, confused, and frightened about their future.

Why? I believe that people are lost in the whirlwind of change and uncertainty. The downsizing phenomenon coupled with corporate greed has done more damage to loyalty than any other paradigm in the history of corporate America. The responsibility for this disconnect must be placed on the shoulders of management, as the quality of performance in any organization is most often a direct reflection of the quality of leadership.

Change is inevitable, but a strong case can be made that we have done a miserable job of managing change. (Gallup found that 71 percent of employees are disengaged at work.) Downsizing, rightsizing, or whatever fancy term is chosen

to justify selfish actions has improved
the bottom line at the expense of wreck-
ing the lives, self-worth, pride, and dignity
of thousands of employees and their
families. All one has to do is reflect on
the Enron and WorldCom scandals of
this decade. The problem is illustrated in
an April 5, 1997, interview with Jeffrey
Skilling—the then president of Enron.
He told the *Seattle Sun Times*, "You must
cut costs ruthlessly by 50 to 60 percent.
Depopulate. Get rid of people. They gum
up the works." History will prove that
this callous disregard of people's worth
will be the greatest obstacle to building
and sustaining healthy corporate
cultures.

But there is good news. The heroes
are the leaders who realize the worth of
people; those who understand the power
of compassion; those who understand
and value the dignity of employees.
These men and women (we need more

women in leadership roles) understand the wisdom of serving others and the positive influence that genuine concern for others has on the balance sheet.

Dare to Lead offers time-tested guidelines for successful leadership. I hope that these insights will encourage and enlighten you on your way to excellence, whether you are a veteran executive looking for a new idea or two or just starting out in your career. Consider *Dare to Lead* your leadership compass, always available to help get you back on track when you find yourself veering off in the wrong direction. These proven ideas will enhance your success whether you are a CEO or a young employee looking for guidance. Good luck in your pursuit of leadership excellence.

DARE TO
LEAD

The Success Triad

The source of most organizational problems is poor communication.

Three Levels of Leadership

Level 1: When people understand you, you get their attention.

Level 2: When people trust you, you earn their loyalty.

Level 3: When people know you really care, you catch their hearts.

Answer the door when opportunity knocks.

Loyalty Formula

Make five deposits of appreciation before you earn the right to *one* withdrawal of criticism.

Avoid the temptation to blame outside circumstances for your problems.

An effective organization functions as a community, not as a family.

Managers hold on; leaders let go.

Why People Control

1. Lack of trust.
2. Lack of confidence.
3. Low self-esteem. "I feel better about me when I control you" attitude.
4. Ego/Arrogance. "I'm better than you" attitude.
5. Perfectionism. "Nobody can do it better than me, so I'll do it myself" attitude. Major reason for burnout.

The weak control, while winners let go.

Eagles will not roost in a sparrow's nest.

The harder you hold on to people and things, the more apt you are to lose them.

Five Steps to Effective Decision-Making:

1. Stop!
2. Ask the right questions of the right people.
3. Listen objectively—with an open mind and heart—to their answers.
4. Think about the consequences of your choices.
5. Respond appropriately.

Constructive anger is the art of not losing your temper.

Leaders ask the right questions to get the right answers.

Be willing to laugh at yourself.

Ten Most Powerful Words

Four Most Powerful: *What do you think?*
Three Most Powerful: *I appreciate you.*
Two Most Powerful: *Thank you.*
Most Powerful: *We.*

Silent and *Listen* have the same letters. Get it?

Leaders visualize **results**.

Vision is the gift of seeing what others only dream.

If you burn your bridges, you'd better be able to walk on water.

First and foremost, a good leader serves others.

Your ability to serve others starts with mastering *yourself*.

Giving associates a chance to demonstrate their skills will develop their confidence.

You can't change anyone. They must take **CARE** of themselves:

Choices they make.
Attitudes they take.
Responsibilities they accept.
Excellence in all thoughts, words, and actions.

O Make finding a solution a higher priority than placing blame.

Seven Cs for Effective Daily Leading:

1. **C**ompetence: learn something new every day.
2. **C**ommunication: ask the right questions.
3. **C**ompassion: make someone feel appreciated.
4. **C**haracter: always do what is right.
5. **C**onnection: plant the seeds of relationships and nourish them with random acts of appreciation.
6. **C**ommitment: be consistently committed to the above.
7. **C**ourage: take responsibility for your life.

Solve today's problems while looking to tomorrow's opportunities.

Respect another's dignity. Never blame or be judgmental.

Surround yourself with talent better than your own and carefully nurture it.

Keep asking questions and listen closely to the answers.

Mistakes are a necessary part of the success process.

Provide the sky in which others can soar.

Goals are dreams with deadlines.

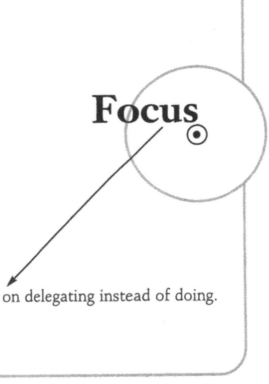

Focus

on delegating instead of doing.

Read *Getting Things Done: The Art of Stress-Free Productivity* by David Allen.

Leaders see more in other people than other people see in themselves.

Milquetoast leadership is *not* the breakfast of champions.

A good plan has a clearly defined objective clearly communicated to everyone.

Praise in public; criticize in **private**.

The Most Dangerous Word

"You did a good job, **but** . . ."

True leaders put the common good ahead of personal gain.

Leaders have an innate ability to bring out the best in others.

Exert your will through **persuasion**, not **intimidation**.

Pursue

Excellence

And

Cherish

Everyone

Most solutions are simple, the
blinding glimpse of the obvious.

Perform for results, not recognition.

Your worst decision is the one that is
never made.

Two Requirements Essential to Achieving One's Full Potential

1. They must be coachable (willing to change).
2. They must be willing to take personal responsibility for their life.

Leaders provide the inspiration. Motivation must come from *within*.

The path to success is often illogical.

"I care about you."
Say it, mean it, and live it.

Decisions should be based on the core values of an organization.

Be willing to **sacrifice**.

A real leader wears **Velcro** instead of Teflon where acceptance of responsibility is concerned.

23

Five Questions That Determine the Health of Your Organization's Culture

1. Are associates treated with dignity and respect?
2. Is management trustworthy?
3. Are opinions both solicited and valued?
4. Is there equity in accountability (same standards from entry level to executive level)?
5. Do people feel appreciated?

How healthy is your culture?

Anticipate chaos and be prepared
to work through it.

Don't get so caught up in the "hairball of
life" that you miss what's important.

Be accessible and accountable.

It's still true—Insanity is continuing the same habits and expecting different results.

Four Steps to a Profitable Enterprise

1. Always do the right thing.
2. Develop people.
3. Pursue excellence.
4. Grow profitability.

Manage yourself; lead others.

A timid employee
is the result of a **tyrant**.

Take charge without always being
in control.

Take initiative and encourage others to do the same.

Beware of shortcuts while looking for ways to minimize the effort needed for desired results.

The worst employees to have on your team are the ones who are not good enough to keep or bad enough to fire. Get rid of them!

A leader has a sense of **humility**.

A leader has a sense of **history**.

A leader has a sense of **humor**.

Use a variety of stories and anecdotes to convey the organization's history and philosophy.

Trust your gut feeling—it's usually right.

True sincerity is a rare but valuable leadership trait.

Practice **R A R E.**
A C E V
N T C E
D S O R
O — G Y
M O N
    F I   D
      T   A
      I   Y
      O
      N

Uncertainties are a part of life. Accept them.

What Real People Say About Real Leaders

"She has the courage to be real. She speaks what's in her heart and doesn't worry if it's politically correct. Her focus is on humanity, not the bottom line. She is the first person in a senior leadership position that I would want to emulate."

"He makes you feel good about yourself without saying anything. He is blessed with the talent of telling you what you need to hear without destroying your spirit. I always feel better about myself after leaving his office."

What are your followers saying about you?

Expect people to perform only as well as the example you set.

Visit each associate's work area at least once a month.

Look for great ideas, not just consensus.

Kindness is not weakness. It is strength under control.

True leadership involves not only the exercise of authority but also full acceptance of responsibility.

Mary Kay's P & L

People and Love

Beware of your blind spots, as what you don't know that you don't know will keep you from developing as a leader.

Look at life through the windshield, not the rearview mirror.

Top Three Reasons Relationships Fail

1. Lack of trust.
2. Lack of communication.
3. Lack of appreciation.

Rewarding relationships start with gratitude and end with lack of trust.

Look to others for information, not decisions.

Be people-serving, not self-serving.

Great leaders understand
The Power of We.

Study the military. There is no
better leadership model.

To lead, one must first learn to follow.

People will follow you if they like you; they won't if they don't.

Watch that EGO!
Edging God Out.

Leadership is a feeling. How do people feel after they leave your presence; after that phone call; after that e-mail?

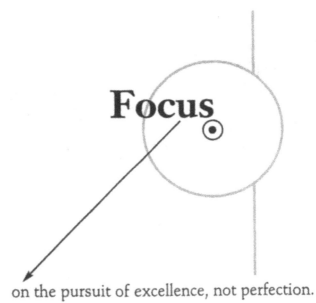

Focus

on the pursuit of excellence, not perfection.

Knowledge is not power.
Knowledge *applied* is power.

Give employees some breathing
room. Be "invisible" one day
every other week.

If you feel that you can't be away
for extended periods of time you
have one of two problems. You
have the wrong team or you're not
a very good leader. Most likely it's
the latter.

P **A** **C** **T**
E C H E
R C A A
S O N M
O U G S
N N E
A T S
L A
B
I
L
I
T
Y

Failure to take a risk is much worse than taking a risk that leads to failure.

Four-Way Test

1. Are you competent?
2. Do you listen to your conscience?
3. Is your character sound?
4. Do you have compassion for others?

If you feel your associates frequently let you down, explore those feelings with your mentor.

Putting ethics into practice involves courage more than conviction.

If you grasp for power, it will slip away.

Leaders understand
the power of **synergy**.

Together teams can achieve greatness; apart they're doomed to mediocrity.

Allow ample time for reflection and dreaming.

Leadership is high-touch versus high-tech.

Always appear calm and cool, never confused.

An in-person visit beats a written memo every time.

Be teachable. You don't know everything.

A genuine show of vulnerability often brings great **rewards**.

Team spirit is simply energy. Is your team's spirit positive or negative?

A good leader is a person of both action and intellect.

Listen to feedback carefully before you respond.

A willingness to encourage change keeps you and your organization moving forward.

Creativity is most often found in the silence of **solitude**. Reserve fifteen minutes a day of uninterrupted quiet time for yourself.

You are as old as your newest idea.

A good leader aspires to be a role model rather than a hero.

Four Characteristics of the World's Most Effective Leaders

1. They care.
2. They believe.
3. They are fair. No double standards.
4. They expect—and will only accept—excellence.

The most important responsibility of a leader is to keep hope alive.

Lead people, not organizations.

If you think you're leading
and no one is following,
you're just taking a **walk**.

Be quick to throw a lifeline to
someone about to be swept under.

Would you want to follow you?

Filter all thoughts through your heart before they become words.

Good leadership is much deeper than personal appearance or rhetoric.

In solving problems, first look for flaws in the organizational structure rather than in the people.

Be aware of an associate's obstacles to success and work together to find the answers.

Integrity and **humility** are the leader's two best friends.

Ask your associates, "What would you do?" Expect powerful results.

Bold leaders choose the playing field over the sidelines.

There are two kinds of pain in life: the pain of discipline and the pain of regret.

Three Keys to Building Winning Teams

1. Find the best talent.
2. Recruit the best talent.
3. Keep the best talent.

Always empower others to do their best.

Set Me Free

If you trust me, set me free.
Don't hold on—let me be.
Hold me, support me, and encourage me,
But set me free.
For if you really care about me,
You will help me achieve
The beautiful rewards
God planned for me.

The greatest gift of life
Is to have my soul set free,
To be that special person
God meant me to be.
For hope is the freedom to see
The beautiful child He crafted in me,
And to live the wonderful life
He created for me.

Love me, but set me free.

Be firm but fair.

Learn to balance logic and emotion.

Realize that a house divided will **fall**.

Organizations that encourage everyone's participation have an inside track to success.

Employees want to be heard and understood.

Learn from failure. Don't be crippled by it.

Your rules apply to you, too.

If you don't love what you do, quit!

Potential results when expressed should fascinate and energize your team.

Every action should have a clear purpose.

There must be a 100 percent commitment to a 51 percent decision.

Employees are the soul of the firm.

Have a genuine concern for those you lead.

Devote your time and energy to **positive** people and **positive** thoughts.

Find your passion and make it work toward the common good.

Put empathy ahead of authority.

Real leaders are **mentors**.

A leader who is willing to share the power enhances consensus decision-making.

Build camaraderie.

Provide others with hope for the future.

A leader living on the edge might unwittingly push others off the cliff.

Together
Excellence
Apart
Mediocrity

Facts of Life

- What you resist persists.
- New habits often occur when the pain of staying the same becomes greater than the pain of change.
- Change is inevitable but growth is optional.
- The winds of change will either blow you away or take you to new heights.

Always keep in mind that what others tell you is only the tip of the iceberg.

You are in partnership with the associates you serve.

Greet everyone with a smile and salutation each morning.

If you choose to chase mice, you'll eventually get trampled by the elephants. **Lesson**: Focus on what's important.

Be cognizant of the unwritten rules that govern the organization.

Put out a suggestion box, read the contents once a week, and act on them.

Illustrate your spoken vision with metaphors.

A leader's state of mind affects every person in the organization.

Be willing and prepared to promote.

You must earn respect, not demand it.

Just because you find a problem doesn't mean the system is broken.

The best concept cannot withstand poor leadership.

Leaders are originals, not duplicates.

Share your joy with **others**.

Develop a spirit of community, one individual at a time.

Leaders often take the unconventional road.

There is no "template" for leaders.

Be there when *needed*, not only when it is convenient.

Roll up your sleeves and get your hands dirty.

True rapport within an organization cannot be developed without a commitment to truth.

A shared philosophy and shared experiences sharpen your team's cohesion.

Consult your conscience.

Choose what is **right** instead of what is politically correct.

The art of persuasion begins with an open mind and open ears, not an open mouth.

Know the difference between a rash decision and a prompt one.

Inside every person are seeds of greatness. Your task is to cultivate them.

Share both the work and the wealth.

Expectations

How good can people be? Their best.
How good should people be? Their best.
How good will people be? Their choice.

Into **self** is a very lonely place.

The quality of performance— employee morale and retention, performance, profitability, etc.—is a direct reflection of the quality of leadership.

Good leaders are like baseball umpires. They go practically unnoticed when doing their job right.

PhD of Leadership
Preserve human Dignity

Accept responsibility for those you lead.

Never put others on the firing line until they are ready.

Tell those you lead what they *need* to hear, not what you think they *want* to hear.

Stand tall through it all.

An apology is the sign of a secure leader.

Enthusiasm is a way of life, not an emotion.

A group of people committed to a shared vision can accomplish the impossible.

Keep in touch with the work being done.

Managers rely on manuals. Leaders rely on instinct.

Walk a mile in another person's shoes before passing judgment. Accept people for who and what they are, regardless of how different they are from you.

Practice what you preach.

The **abuse** of power and people will eventually result in **failure**.

Tackle problems by helping associates choose the solution.

No PGA!
Power Greed & Arrogance.
Remember Enron¿

Power – "I need to control."
Greed – "I want it all."
Arrogance – "I know it all."

The pursuit of perfection will destroy morale.

We are what we watch, listen to, and read.

If you don't love people, you will never lead them.

Learn from the past, focus on the present, and prepare for the **future**.

What people think, say, or do—to or about you—rarely has anything to do with you. It's typically a reflection of how they feel about themselves.

If all you focus on is winning, you won't.

CEO – **C**hief **E**ntertainment **O**fficer

The only known constant of the present and the future is people. Focus your energy on finding and keeping the best and they will take care of the rest.

Make important decisions only when you are alert and relaxed.

An open-door policy should be exactly that.

Continually develop your character and your competence.

Coercion kills the corporate spirit.

Realize that knowledge and skill are of no value without the fuel of **motivation**.

Encourage change and new ideas. Don't be intimidated by them.

The effective leader instills commitment to—not mere compliance with—the shared vision.

Culture Commandments
Winning Values = Winning Cultures

1. We will treat one another with dignity and respect.
2. We will praise the accomplishments of one another.
3. We will speak kind words to one another.
4. We will be encouragers.
5. We will seek—and *speak*—the truth.
6. We will focus on *what's* right and not worry about *who's* right.
7. We will listen to learn.
8. We will smile and have a healthy sense of humor.
9. We will not gossip.
10. We will expect excellence in all thoughts, words, and actions.

Team Rule #1 – We will hold one another accountable to live the above.

Take your full vacation time!

Continue to work on your communication skills—both written and verbal.

Establish a **Personal Board of Directors**. Select those who you admire for their success and character. Most importantly, choose those who will tell you what you need to hear.

Take what you've got and make what you've got better.

Remember to accept losing with dignity.

Each week select two items from your to-do list and delegate them to a capable employee.

Help people produce results they can be proud of personally.

A soft word turns away anger.

Use "we" instead of "me."

Your personality is what people think you are. Your character is what you are.

Set priorities and live by them.

Listen with your heart
as well as your **head**.

Employees want to be heard
and understood.

Relationships Health Quiz

1. Do people enjoy being with you?
2. Do people trust you?
3. Do people feel comfortable sharing their feelings without fear of retribution?
4. Do you listen without judging or offering advice?
5. Do you tell people what they need to hear, not necessarily what they want to hear?
6. Does time spent with you improve the quality of lives?
7. Do you drain or energize people's spirits?
8. Do people feel better after spending time with you?

How healthy are your relationships?

Encourage decision-making at all levels.

Give others the freedom to fail. Far too many refuse to take risks for fear of the ramifications.

Share—don't hide—your knowledge with associates.

Small changes often produce big results.

Are leaders born or made? My answer: you can't give a person what God left out.

Use your drive time to and from work to listen to motivational tapes.

A good decision today beats the "perfect" decision next week.

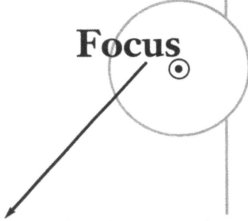

Focus

on strengths and manage weaknesses.

The path of least resistance is not always the best choice.

Never use others for self-gain.

A true leader trains others to lead.

Be courteous.

Emulate the leadership habits of Vince Lombardi: discipline, hard work, and commitment.

If necessary, agree to disagree.

Always focus on the big picture.

Understand and support the highest priorities of others.

True loyalty is only that which is volunteered.

Be consistently authentic and genuine. If you lose people's trust, it's almost impossible to regain it.

Eat properly.

Don't feel you have to do it all yourself.

Keep a journal and write in it **daily**.

Learn to tap into the power of **silence**.

Examine your health consistently.

Develop meaningful relationships
at every level.

Watch out for the "squeaky wheel."

Reward performance, not need.

Good leaders are not control freaks.

Envision goals as the targets and habits as the arrows.

Effective leaders are benevolent dictators—they guard and reinforce their values.

PC of Leadership

Passion for what you do and Compassion for those you serve.

Never carry a grudge.

Give others credit for your **success.**

The best concept cannot withstand poor leadership.

Offer incentives that encourage others to take risks.

Passionate hearts committed to a shared vision can accomplish the impossible.

How to effectively **L E A D**

L E A R N

E D U C A T E

A P P R E C I A T E

D E V E L O P

Be flexible.

Instill confidence, not confusion, in those you lead.

Avoid the quick **fix**.

The level of perceived appreciation is the most reliable predictor of success.

Recommended Reading on Leadership

- *Synchronicity* – Joseph Jaworski
- *The Living Company* – Arie de Geus
- *First, Break All the Rules* – Marcus Buckingham and Curt Coffman
- *Now, Discover Your Strengths* – Marcus Buckingham and Donald Clifton
- *Soar with Your Strengths* – Donald Clifton and Paula Nelson
- *On Becoming a Servant Leader: The Private Writings of Robert K. Greenleaf* – Don Frick and Larry Spears, editors
- *The Five Dysfunctions of a Team* – Patrick Lencioni

- *Leadership Is an Art* – Max DePree
- *Nuts! The Story of Southwest Airlines* – Kevin and Jackie Freiberg
- *The Soul of the Firm* – William Pollard
- *Well Done!* – Dave Thomas
- *You Can Have It All* – Mary Kay Ash
- *Made in America* – Sam Walton

Leaders look at others as equals, not as subordinates.

Respect those you serve.

Before you critique another's behavior, list five positive things about that person.

Employees who are given positive feedback work harder and accomplish more.

Look for ways to make other people's jobs more challenging *and* fulfilling.

Leadership Is Just Common Sense

- College gives knowledge; life gives wisdom.
- College gives answers; life gives the questions.
- College focuses on success; life teaches significance.
- College teaches management; life teaches leadership.

Perhaps we should call it "good sense," since it isn't very common!

You must be yourself to be at peace.

Instead of thinking, "I have to go to work," think, "I get to."

ACT – **A**ction **C**hanges **T**hings.

Genuine friendship can't exist where one of the parties is unwilling to hear the truth, and the other is equally indisposed to speak it.

—Cicero

Small acts of recognition are very important.

Understand the fragility and importance of others' self-esteem.

Follow the channels of authority and remember that it works both ways.

A Leader

I went on a search to become a leader. I searched high and low. I spoke with authority. People listened. But alas, there was one who was wiser than I, and they followed that individual.

I sought to inspire confidence, but the crowd responded, "Why should I trust you?"

I postured and assumed the look of leadership with a countenance that flowed with confidence and pride. But many passed me by and never noticed my air of elegance.

I ran ahead of the others, pointing the way to new heights. I demonstrated that I knew the route to greatness. And then I looked back and I was alone.

"What shall I do?" I queried. "I've tried hard and used all that I know." And I sat down and pondered long.

And then, I listened to the voices around me. And I heard what the group was trying to accomplish. I rolled up my sleeves and joined in the work.

As we worked, I asked, "Are we all

together in what we want to do and how to get the job done؟"

And we thought together and we fought together and we struggled toward our goal.

I found myself encouraging the faint-hearted. I sought the ideas of those too shy to speak out. I taught those who had little skill. I praised those who worked hard. When our task was completed, one of the group turned to me and said, "This would not have been done but for your leadership."

At first I said, "I didn't lead. I just worked with the rest." And then I understood that leadership is not a goal. It's a way to reach a goal.

I lead best when I help others to go where we've decided to go. I lead best when I help others to use themselves creatively. I lead best when I forget about myself as a leader and focus on my group—their needs and their goals. To lead is to serve . . . to give . . . to achieve together.

– Anonymous

The things that will destroy us are:
Politics without principle;
Pleasure without conscience;
Wealth without work;
Knowledge without character;
Business without morality;
Science without humanity,
And worship without sacrifice.
—Anonymous

Communication is the lifeblood of trust.

The vision of the leader is the hope of the pack.

Focus on guiding, not ruling.

Exercise regularly.

Seek wise **counsel**.

Be real. Others know when you're just going through the motions of good leadership.

Change three bad habits a year—
you will get phenomenal results!

Send everyone home two hours early—
with full pay—one day next week.

The harder a leader pushes,
the more he or she pulls the
organization down.

An organization's value is
measured as much by the meaning
it has for its employees as it is by
net profits.

Give others the benefit of the doubt.

Willingly spend extra time with those who want to **improve**.

Leadership is about stewardship, not ownership.

No decision should be made in isolation.

A healthy organization improves the lives of its individuals.

Learn how to help others achieve their full potential.

Mother Teresa's Leadership Wisdom

The fruit of silence is **prayer**.
The fruit of prayer is **faith**.
The fruit of faith is **love**.
The fruit of love is **service**.
The fruit of service is **peace**.

F A I T H
Faith Always Is The Hero

Accept blame as well as fame.

Continue to find new ways to support those around you.

Do not lower your standards to accommodate others.

Be willing to create openings for exceptional people, even when a position isn't currently available.

Be willing to forgive yourself, too.

Failure sends a leader in a new direction toward his or her next **success**.

Learn from the past, but don't be paralyzed by it.

The past doesn't have a future, but you do.

Recommended Movies

- *Radio*
- *Miracle*
- *Remember the Titans*
- *Rudy*
- *Music of the Heart*
- *October Sky*
- *Forrest Gump*

A prudent leader understands the risk/reward relationship.

Be willing to swim upstream.

Think of work as an adventure
and instill a sense of exploration in
others.

Look for ways to relieve stress
in those around you.

A reprimand should build up, not tear down.

Realize that we live in the real world, not an ideal one.

Lead a balanced life—faith, family, work—and encourage the same in those you lead.